I Love My Love

A Play

Fay Weldon

A SAMUEL FRENCH ACTING EDITION

FOUNDED 1830

SAMUELFRENCH-LONDON.CO.UK
SAMUELFRENCH.COM

CHARACTERS

Derek
Cat
Mark
Anne
Lynn

The action takes place in Devon and London

ACT I SCENE 1 The Village Shop
SCENE 2 The Studio
SCENE 3 The Village Shop
SCENE 4 The Studio
SCENE 5 The Village Shop

ACT II SCENE 1 The Farmhouse Kitchen and City Apartment
SCENE 2 The City Apartment
SCENE 3 The Farmhouse Kitchen
SCENE 4 The City Apartment
SCENE 5 The Farmhouse Kitchen
SCENE 6 The City Apartment
SCENE 7 The Railway Station

Time—the present

I Love My Love was first presented on Radio 3 and subsequently at the Orange Tree, Richmond.

AUTHOR'S NOTE

THE CAST

Derek is in his late thirties; a country-man, slow, honest, powerful, pleasant in appearance and deed. A good man and an admirable father.
Anne is in her middle thirties, practical and bright. A good, hard-working, virtuous wife.
Mark is in his middle-thirties; nervy, ambitious, attractive and worldly.
Cat hovers about thirty, sleek, seductive and idle.
This, at least, is how we can describe our characters at the beginning of the play. By the end a good deal of personality-swapping has occurred.
Lynn is a journalist, in her mid-twenties. She appears at the end of Act I and is not seen again.

THE SETS

The village shop, the design studio, the city flat, the country kitchen, the railway station—appears at the very end of Act II as a postscript. These backgrounds can be as simple or as elaborate as suits the production.

ACT I

The Village Shop

It's snowing. Derek's at the counter, stock-taking. Cat is at the sardine shelf, checking numbers. She's dressed for town, not country, and must be rather chilly. Derek surveys her

Derek I love my love with an A because she is admirable.

Cat —thirty-four, thirty-five——

Derek I hate my love with an A because she is argumentative.

Cat —forty, forty-one———

Derek (*changing his mind*) Her name is Anthea. She comes from Albania.

Cat Well, that lets me out. Forty-four, forty-five——

Derek (*hopefully*) I gave her an aspidistra.

Cat You would. Now I've lost count.

Derek There is no need to count the sardines, Cat.

Cat It is part of the bargain. I am perfectly sure your wife would be stock-taking at this moment. Filling the flying hours, counting the sardines.

Derek No. We'd be passing the time in other ways.

Cat (*with gritted teeth*) Very well, if that's how it is. No sardines.

Derek Because we're past filling time, now, you see. We're on to passing time. It begins to look as if the snow plough won't be here for some hours. They either start this end of the village, or that, and I'm afraid by now it's that.

Cat What a quaint little out-of-the-way-village it is, to be sure. Old-world. Why don't they get another snow plough?

Derek They can't afford it.

Cat So what do we do to pass the time?

Derek Anne and I would play I love my love.

Cat Is it dangerous?

Derek It's a child's game. But we like it. That's why I gave you an aspidistra. I rather think you gave it back.

Cat I'm sorry. I didn't realize. So, let's play I love my love.

Derek You don't have to go on behaving so well, Cat. You can be yourself now. The week's up. You'd be home if it wasn't for the snow. An Act of God. So I reckon the life-swap's over. You've earned your thousand pounds.

Cat Oh no. I'll see it through to the end. The very end. God must have meant something. (*As a polite little girl*) Really, I've had a perfectly enjoyable time, Derek, thank you very much. You were very good to me: kind and courteous and helpful. It's been such an interesting experiment, hasn't it?—and I do admire your wife. She's obviously so efficient: all those jars of blackberry jam. I've never had the *jam* before, only the jelly, without the pips. And I really have tried to step into her shoes—well, her wellies—as I'm sure she's stepped into mine. I don't regret it at all, it's just I hadn't reckoned on snow in March: I thought spring in the country was supposed to be primroses. After a winter in the city, and flu, and one thing and another, I'd looked forward to a week in the country, hedgerows, and birdsong and primroses. Well, I expect the snow plough won't be all that long. And then I can get to the station.

Derek Do put on a woollie: you're shivering.

Cat No, I'm not. And of course Mark being a friend of the girl on the magazine. *Femina*. Quite a good friend, I think. We have an open marriage, you see. Not like you and Anne, obviously. Anyway, Mark was very keen on my doing it, for one reason and another. And a thousand pounds—well! So I said OK to the girl from *Femina*; your readers want a life-swap story, I won't disappoint them, or Mark. So I did it. I changed places with another woman: I lived her life, washed her floors, swept back her mud, fuelled her Aga, fed her goats and her dogs and her cats and her hens. And her children. And her husband. Chatted to her friends about recipes. For a week. A whole week. I didn't know time went so slowly in the country. All I wouldn't do was wear her clothes.

Derek Found your tongue, at last. Well, it wasn't too bad, was it? Hard work, of course. I don't supposed you're used to that. Anne will have had quite a holiday. But you learned from us, and we learned from you.

Cat Naturally. That was the idea. Me to learn from you. And to increase *Femina's* circulation, of course, by self-revelation!

Derek Don't be cynical. It doesn't suit you.

Cat And don't you patronize me. Why does the snow go sideways? I thought it was supposed to fall from top to bottom.

Derek It's a blizzard. Fine snow and a high wind. That's why we're getting all these drifts. I'm afraid it means hardship for a lot of people. Not just us.

Cat Of course. I'm thinking of that. Shall we open a bottle of whiskey?

Derek Whiskey!

Cat Oh God. Sherry, then.

Derek Well, why not. In the circumstances. There's some Bristol Cream beneath the cider. In the drink section. We keep it rather small. We don't want to encourage the youngsters.

Cat Youngsters? Are there any? Does it have to be Bristol Cream?

Derek It's our best seller.

Cat That figures.

Derek And of course it has to be paper cups.

Cat Of course.

Derek I love my love with a C because she is content. I hate her because she is cantankerous.

Cat Stop getting at me.

Derek I'm not. I just have a speculative mind, that's all.

Cat I hadn't noticed it.

Derek I don't mean to hurt you, or patronize you, or any of the things you say I have. I have tried to be polite, and helpful, and friendly.

Cat Yes, you have. You've been very kind. It made me uneasy. I'm not used to it.

Derek I'm sure your husband is kind to you.

Cat That's not quite the word for it.

Derek But we weren't supposed to get too personal, were we? Avoid comparisons. Of course, the week's over. We're in injury time, in a way.

Cat Their very respectable swap. Well, it's a very respectable magazine. Mark's agency buys a lot of space in it. You do them a good turn, they do you a good turn. You get your name in the columns, they get more customers, it's all good for business Mark says. Well, he's right. You know how it is.

Derek We just wanted a thousand pounds and a new roof—God knows what this blizzard is doing to it. At least the children are with my mother.

Cat Thoughts of home. Always your mind turns to thoughts of home.

Derek Doesn't everyone's?

Cat No.

Derek What does yours turn to?

Cat Sex.

Derek I beg your pardon?

Cat It's ridiculous. Do a life-swap. Me and Anne. Her to the city, me to the country. Her to theatres and parties, me to the kids and the hens. She's supposed to win, you know. Everyone wants to prove me shoddy and empty, and they probably will, because of what's been left out. The only thing we're not supposed to do. Change sleeping partners.

Derek I should hope not. Anne and I would never ever have considered it. It's not a pornographic magazine.

Cat You won't even think about it. It didn't even enter your mind all week.

Derek No.

Cat I find that insulting, frankly.

Derek Shall we change the subject?

Cat No. I bet it entered Mark's head. But I expect Anne was wearing her wellies, and he isn't into wellies.

Silence

Derek It is rather cold in here. Shall I turn up the oil-fire?

Cat It will only smell and smoke and blacken the ceiling.

Derek Please, put on one of Anne's jerseys. There, on a shelf to the back of the paper-cups. Over there, where the party stationery is.

Cat Party stationery? What's that?

Derek Muppet tablecloths and doilies and jelly moulds.

Cat Yes. I went to a party, didn't I? In the church hall. What a wow that was.

Derek You behaved very well. I was proud of you. A lot of people move away from Mrs Beale when she starts shouting. Her deaf-aid plays up.

Cat I was stunned. I couldn't move. This one? The khaki double knit?

Derek That's it. Anne's had that since we were first married. Twelve years.

Cat She wasn't married in it?
Derek Stop that.
Cat Sorry. (*She puts it on*) How's that?
Derek Better.

SCENE 2

The Studio

Mark's at a drawing board. Anne is acting as a model; she leans against a screen, brilliantly lit. Her clothes cover her more than adequately

Mark It's very good of you to do this.
Anne Not at all. It's part of the bargain.
Mark The week is over. You've more than earned the thousand pounds.
Anne It's been so easy.
Mark Has it?
Anne Yes. And standing here against a screen is counted as work?
Mark Yes. In a way. Helping at the studio. Well, not helping, because that sounds as if the woman takes a subsidiary role, which is not Cat's and my way. We split the chores. Sensible division of labour, is what we go in for. I draw better than Cat, so I'm the artist. She looks better, so she gets drawn. Of course she doesn't wear quite so many clothes as you.
Anne I'm afraid that's just me.
Mark Yes. I'd noticed that.
Anne I'm surprised she doesn't catch cold.
Mark The place is warm enough. Isn't it?
Anne More than warm. Central heating is very irritating to the mucous membrane of the throat and lungs and predisposes to infection. Fires are more healthy.
Mark And messier.
Anne Of course, the difference is, as I've realized, Derek and I see the home as our life. It's what we do, so we don't mind taking time and trouble over it. You see the home as a background to your life, so you like to get the chores over and out as quickly as possible.
Mark But of course.
Anne To save time.
Mark Yes.
Anne But what do you do with the time? When do you *live*?
Mark You can hardly enjoy scrubbing floors.
Anne I do.
Mark But what about your hands?
Anne Honest hands. Hard-working. Loving.
Mark Cat models rings, sometimes.
Anne I expect she does.
Mark So what are you going to tell the magazine about your week here?
Anne That I'm glad to get home. That I had fun, but the real life's back there.
Mark Do you think Cat's slept with your husband?

Anne What an extraordinary thing to say.

Mark Do you?

Anne Of course she hasn't.

Mark Why shouldn't she?

Anne Because he wouldn't. It wouldn't enter his head. He's married to me and we're serious people. You don't shock me. I just think you're being silly.

Mark I wasn't trying to shock you. Just stir your complacency. Cat's a very attractive woman.

Anne I haven't met her, but I'm sure she is. As for complacency, you have such a twisted view of things, such a peculiar life style, complacency is the only word you can find for ordinary self-respect.

Mark You weren't like this during the week.

Anne No. I smiled, I nodded, I did my best. I shopped at your ridiculous delicatessen, where your wife is robbed daily. I bought sheets at Harrods, I had my hair messed up at the hairdresser, I served your smart friends alcohol, I wrote a letter to your poor little son, away at school, I lunched with the most extraordinary boring people, went to see crude and silly paintings and deafened myself with shrieks and wails from your stereophonic sound system, which has, I may say, been very badly set up. I held my tongue. The week is over and we're into injury time.

Mark I don't notice you rushing home.

Anne I can't get home. The station's snowed in. If it's as bad as that there, the road to the farmhouse will be impassable for days, and the shop will be cut off. I can't get home. Thank God the children are with my mother. So I'll hold the fort for you until your wife can get back. Don't bother to thank me, it's the least I can do. When an Act of God befalls, the least people can do is stick together.

Mark You're quite funny sometimes. If you'd take off one of your jerseys I could get the curve of the arm right.

Anne I wear what I wear. I expect it's a sexist drawing, anyway. I don't want to be party to it.

Mark It's a drawing of an elderly woman for a medical ad. She's got arthritis, and she can't reach the lavatory chain. Headline—"when ordinary life must stop". It has to be a drawing, because a photograph would be too gruesome, in the circumstances.

Anne Your life is one long euphemism, I notice. The avoidance of reality.

Mark No. It's a making of allowances for human nature. Do you really like living in the country?

Anne Yes.

Mark You don't just think you ought to?

Anne No.

Mark Must be dreadful when the roof leaks.

Anne It is. That's why I did this life-swap.

Mark My experience is, people often use money as an excuse. They do what they want, but claim they do it for the money.

Anne It's true, life gets a little, well, everyday down there. But the values are right.

Mark Yes, of course. This is just froth and bubble.
Anne Yes.
Mark Not like shutting the hens in for the night. In a snowstorm.
Anne No.
Mark That's really living.
Anne Yes.
Mark Do you believe in God?
Anne Of course.
Mark Go to Church?
Anne Of course.
Mark So Cat will have gone, on Sunday.
Anne I certainly hope so. Do her good.
Mark What do you mean by that? You don't know her. You've never met her.
Anne I don't mean to criticize her.
Mark Yes, you do.
Anne I'm not that kind of person.
Mark My impression of you is that you have no idea what kind of person you are.
Anne Now there'll be a lot of Freudian clap-trap about identity and motivation.
Mark Christ. Look, shut-up and take off the jersey. Please.

Anne takes off the jersey

That's better.

She's silent. He works for a little

It's cold in here. I hope to God the central heating hasn't packed up.
Anne I turned it off. It's very bad for you. Stuffy and hot. You need someone to look after you, not indulge your whims. That's what proper love is.

Mark puts down his charcoal and goes off in search of the whiskey

And you've had far too much to drink today already.

He advances as if to hit her

You'll rot your brain cells. You'll become violent and stupid. That may be what's the matter with you already. Look at you! Your wit fails you. That's what drink does. You will think you are being charming when you are really being silly. You will think people admire you when actually they are sorry for you. Because you won't be able to help it: you will be a drunk. An alcoholic.

His arm falls

Mark Are you like this with your husband?
Anne Of course not. There's no need. We never have rows.
Mark Perhaps you never tell him what to do.
Anne No. I don't.
Mark Then why do you tell me what to do all the time?

Anne Because you need someone to look after you.

Mark Then take off all your clothes and come and look after me.

Anne There you go again. That sort of silliness. I am trying to be serious, and you take refuge in stupidity.

Mark Don't you think sex is serious?

Anne I think it's serious in a way you couldn't possibly begin to understand. I love my husband, and I'm sure Cat loves you, and I wish you were more loyal to her. You show yourself in a very bad light.

Mark Oh, Christ.

Anne And swearing is just silly, too. Especially if you don't believe in God. What's the point? Get on with the drawing.

He does

An elderly arthritic woman reaching for the toilet chain.

Mark Yes.

Anne Would you have asked Cat to pose for this?

Mark No.

This silences Anne. Presently she takes off another cardigan. He does not respond, but draws on

SCENE 3

The Village Shop

Rain falls; snow swirls. Snow ploughs rumble in the distance, the shouts of workmen are heard, approaching; passing. The snow falls vertically, rather than horizontally. The shop seems warmer and cosier than before. Derek's making up orders, packing them into a cardboard box: Cat's running up and down the shelves, fetching items as he lists them

Derek One box of Twining's Breakfast and a forty-eight of Typhoo tips. Four packs of Jaffa Cakes, and three of All Bran. Thanks. White self-raising three pound bag. Careful it's not split. It's the General. He's particular. Well, his daughter is. I love my love with an O because she is old. The gardener ran off with the General's wife.

Cat He didn't.

Derek He did. The General's wife was sixty and the gardener was thirty. He was married.

Cat Perhaps the General's wife knew a thing or two the gardener's wife didn't.

Derek That's rather a vulgar thing to say.

Cat Not at all. And I must be able to say what comes into my head, without you finding fault. Why do you think he ran off with her?

Derek Because they fell in love.

Cat Perhaps that's the same thing.

Derek Sex and love are not the same thing. I'm sorry for you if you think they are. Drinking chocolate, please, large.

Cat Is that for the General's daughter, so she gets a good night's sleep?
Derek I expect so.
Cat Pity she can't have the gardener.
Derek She's a good girl and a great comfort to her father.
Cat So she should be.
Derek Eight tins of baked beans.
Cat Yuk.
Derek Cheap and nourishing. I'm quite enjoying this.
Cat So am I.
Derek Better than during the week. Why do you think that is?
Cat Things are out in the open, that's why.
Derek What things?
Cat You fancying me.
Derek I never said that.
Cat How could you help it. Anne wearing wellies, day and night.
Derek She does nothing of the kind.
Cat There were enough wellies in the house for twenty wives.
Derek There are always more wellies than feet in a house. I never know why. Of course men lust after women in their hearts; that doesn't mean they don't love their wives.
Cat Perhaps it does.
Derek You go too far. Cornflakes, large, and two Weetabix.
Cat Did you want to have a shop?
Derek It seemed a sensible thing to do.
Cat I said, did you want to have a shop?
Derek No.
Cat What did you want to do?
Derek I wanted to sell the farmhouse, and move to Portugal and live in the sun on the capital for the rest of our lives.
Cat Then why didn't you?
Derek Because it wasn't sensible.
Cat Who said so?
Derek Anne. But she was right: it wasn't sensible.
Cat Why not?
Derek There were the children.
Cat The children could have gone to Portugese schools.
Derek Hardly.
Cat Why not.
Derek It was just an idea. It wasn't practical.
Cat Our lives are made up of ideas. Whose idea were the children?
Derek They just happened.
Cat Anne's idea. Why do her ideas come true, not yours?
Derek You haven't even met Anne. If you had, you would appreciate her. Of course you didn't wear her clothes. I'm glad you didn't. You weren't worthy of them.
Cat Oh, worthy! Who wants to go to bed with worthy.

His turn now, to want to strike her. She laughs. She puts on a cardigan of Anne's—mustardy-yellow

Better? Why did you marry her? Did she say that was sensible?
Derek Yes, and so it was. I wanted to.
Cat Was the farmhouse her idea or yours?
Derek Both.
Cat It needed a lot of work, I imagine.
Derek Yes. It's very enjoyable, making something out of nothing.
Cat Must have been difficult to concentrate on it all, when you were working in the Education Department.
Derek For a time, it was.
Cat Quite a relief when you were redundant.
Derek Yes.
Cat Quite a relief for the department, I expect. You must have arrived worn out, after the house, after the goats. Taking them up to the field every morning. Anne's goats.
Derek She's not physically strong enough. Erica's very stubborn. She has to be pulled up and pushed back. And she's bad-tempered. If she butts you in the groin you limp for weeks.
Cat Why don't you sell her?
Derek Because we don't want her to go to someone who doesn't understand her.
Cat Who doesn't? Anne? You mean you love those goats?
Derek I hate them.
Cat And the hens.
Derek We get wonderfully fresh new-laid eggs. That's important for the children.
Cat All eggs have the same nutritional value, no matter what the hen's lifestyle.
Derek I didn't know that.
Cat I don't suppose Anne told you.
Derek I don't want to be told things by Anne.
Cat Yes you do.
Derek You are trying to turn me against Anne. It won't work. I know all these things. I know what I have given up. A man does give up freedom when he marries.
Cat It depends who he marries. Mark hasn't given up his freedom.
Derek Then it isn't marriage.
Cat An open marriage. We're both sexually free: we're good companions, lovers: just not exclusive.
Derek Whose idea was that?
Cat Mark's.
Derek Of course.
Cat But he's right. No-one ever is faithful, for ever; so why be hypocritical?
Derek You're wrong. People are faithful to one another. They commit themselves, and that's that. And what is this freedom you talk about? Freedom for what?
Cat Life's so short. You have to use it while you can.
Derek You think that because you live in the city. Life seems long to me. Long and deep, like a river. Don't you want him to be faithful to you?

Cat Yes.

Derek Don't you want to be faithful to him?

Cat No.

Derek That's because there's no commitment. I'm sorry for you.

Cat You're sorry for me?

Derek Yes.

Cat Oh God. Let's just get on with the General's order.

Derek It's finished. It's Miss Rose now. She's a senior citizen. Quarter pound pack each of cheese, butter and bacon. She had a daughter when she was fifty-two. A first child.

Cat I don't believe you.

Derek She said it was an Immaculate Conception. I love my love with an H because it is heavenly.

Cat What did the village say?

Derek They went along with it. A tin of frankfurters in brine.

Cat All the same you were shocked when you were made redundant; Anne was happy enough about it: it kept you nearer to her. You had to take this shop: it was all you could do, and you hate it, every minute of it. You make the best of it, because that's in your nature. But your marriage is unhappy.

Derek No.

Cat Yes it is. I have lived in your house for a week, and though the wood stoves are burning, and she makes home-made bread, and wine out of damsons, she is trying too hard. The sheets are cold. I can feel it.

Derek I've said nothing.

Cat You don't have to.

Derek This wasn't part of the bargain.

Cat Yes it was. It was. She would never have gone, I would never have come, if we hadn't wanted it. Change. Life-swap. Trying out another woman's clothes. Well, we did it. She deserted you. Went to another man as his wife.

Derek Not to his bed.

Cat How do you know?

Derek Because I do.

Cat Exactly. Because she's cold, and you're warm, and you are wasting your life when there is so much pleasure to be had from it. Look at me.

Derek Women like you are two a penny.

Cat And what do you think you are? You're frightened of yourself, and your nature; and you're frightened of competition, you're wounded, and she won't even put a bandage on.

Derek I don't understand you. Do you hate her, or do you love me?

Cat Love? Who said anything about love? I'm talking about sex. You said yourself they were different.

Derek I suppose no-one would ever know.

Cat You are ignoble. They have made you so ignoble.

Derek I don't mean it like that. I mean, things only happen if they are observed to happen. Otherwise, it might just as well be in the imagination. Where it certainly has been.

Cat All week?

Derek All week.

Cat What a waste. What a wicked waste. Seven lonely nights in a damp high
bed, with linoleum on the floor, and the thought of how cold your toes will
be when you put your feet out in the morning. You don't have to live like
that.

Derek No.

Cat You could do what you want. You could live in Portugal.

Derek No. Too late.

Cat It's never too late to do what one wants. Only courage fails.

Derek I couldn't leave wife, children, home, shop. Everything.

Cat You could. All you would have to do, is agree to be wicked. And before
you had Anne, you had your mother, and all they ever said to you, was this,
and this, and this, was how a man should live. And so you did. And where
is your manhood now?

*That just about does it. He doesn't stand a chance, in the face of this seasoned
seductress*

You were not born gentle. I know you were not.

Meanwhile

SCENE 4

The Studio

*Anne, now in still fewer woollies, has given up posing. She looks through racks
of lay-outs, and peers through enlargers. Mark has the whiskey bottle out. She
seems to have stopped worrying about that*

Anne But where do you see this kind of life leading?

Mark More money, prettier girls, faster cars.

Anne How vulgar.

Mark I knew you'd say that. Accomplishment, then. The respect of
colleagues. I'd like to do a campaign or so before I die, that people
remember. Mark Madden, they'll say. Oh yes, a great advertising man.

Anne Do they say that kind of thing?

Mark Yes.

Anne And Cat? What does she want to be remembered by?

Mark I think Cat just wants to have a good time. That's why I like her. We
get drunk together: eat good meals together: are rude to waiters and get
flung out of bars together.

Anne Do you love her?

Mark I don't know. If she wasn't there I'd soon find out. That's the only way
you ever know, I find.

Anne I love my love with an A because she is absent.

Mark What?

Anne Just a game Derek and I play: when we have time to spare. Or when
we're driving with the children abroad. We go camping every year, you
know.

Mark That figures.

Anne I hate it, but Derek loves it.

Mark Why do you do what you don't want?

Anne That's life, isn't it.

Mark Not mine, it isn't.

Anne It's all doing what you don't want, so far as I can see. I didn't want to do this life-swap but Derek insisted. I knew I'd hate it. He said how else would we ever get the roof fixed. And it's true the shop doesn't bring in as much as we hoped. And we have all these health foods, but people are very slow to adopt new ideas, even when their own interests are at stake. Had you noticed that?

Mark Yes, I certainly had.

Anne And how can I possibly sleep with you? I'd feel ridiculous. I'm not even that sort of person.

Mark You're quite right. But why not? You're the same height, build and weight as Cat. If I look at your features one by one, they are fair enough. But put them all together, and something's missing.

Anne I do find sex rather embarrassing.

Mark I wish Cat did.

Anne Why?

Mark She's very free with her favours. Too free.

Anne There's a girl in our village like that. She's anyone's. Other people's husbands are always going off to live with her. They give her babies; then they go away. She's ever such a slut. Dirty and smelly. But some men seem to like that. I must say I was disgusted by what I found behind Cat's fridge.

Mark What did you find?

Anne Dirt.

Mark Then why look?

Anne Everything. Pools of sour milk, and old sausages, and jam and mice droppings, and butter paper and a whole packet of paper clips spilled. I cleaned everything in my house before I did this life-swap. I'd have been ashamed not to. It's not as if she had a lot to do, either.

Mark Don't criticize Cat. She's my wife.

Anne She's a thoroughly bad wife.

Mark But I like her.

Anne She's idle.

Mark She has a lovely figure.

Anne It is exactly the same as mine. And I don't use mine as any sort of justification. I hope she hasn't been giving my children junk food.

Mark She will, if it saves trouble.

Anne She was supposed to give them the same kind of meals I did. It was part of the bargain. I did my best for you. Taramasalata. Ugh!

Mark You could have bought it from the take-away. It's only downstairs.

Anne You can make it for a tenth of the price.

Mark But why? No point in saving. Inflation eats everything away. The only possible reaction to the economic situation is eat now think later.

Anne I rang the farm but the lines were down. I hope Derek's all right.

Mark He's got my Cat to keep him warm.

Anne Don't start that.

Mark You're worried now. I've shaken you.

Anne He's very impressionable.

Mark He's a weak man.

Anne What makes you say that?

Mark That's why you're such a strong woman.

Anne I don't want to be a strong woman.

Mark He couldn't even keep down a job.

Anne He didn't enjoy it. He kept falling asleep at his desk. He was bored.

Mark So now you're married to a shopkeeper.

Anne It's a very useful thing to be.

Mark But you don't want to be useful. You want to be like Cat. Useless.

Anne It's too late. I have all these things to keep going. That great big house, with its stoves and its open fires, and the children home for lunch because school dinners are such poisonous stodge and the goats and the hens and my mother-in-law, the Village Society and the shop, and Derek works so slowly, you've no idea, and I'm so bored I think I'm going to die, and when is it ever going to stop?

Mark Here and now.

Anne You don't love me. You don't even like me.

Mark I admire you. Yes I do.

Anne Even when I describe my life to you it appears ridiculous.

Mark That's because you define yourself by what you do, not by what you are. That's why life swaps are always so unsatisfactory. You can't change what you are, by what you do. By changing your accessories.

Anne Then how can people ever improve themselves? How can society get better?

Mark It can't. That's why we have to have a good time now.

Anne I know what it is. You think your wife has been sleeping with my husband, so you want to get even by sleeping with me. Well, I'm not going to be used like that. It is ridiculous to think of Derek making love to anyone except me. Especially not to someone like Cat.

Mark Why not?

Anne Because he's so bad at it, that's why. And someone like her wouldn't look at someone like him.

Mark Now that's not a nice way to speak of the man you love. And besides, you haven't met her. How do you know what she's like?

Anne She doesn't sound to me the kind of woman who thinks warmth and loving murmurs is enough.

Mark You never know. You just never know. Everyone wants something different.

Anne What do you want?

Mark Love. Who doesn't?

Anne How could I possibly love you? I don't admire you.

Mark Do you admire your husband?

Anne Of course. He's a very good man. Brave and kind, and responsible and caring. When I look round at the dreadful time most women have, I realize

I am the luckiest of women. Everyone in the village says so. Our marriage is solid as a rock.

Mark Do you love him?

Anne No.

Mark Well then.

SCENE 5

The Village Shop

In the shop, in the meanwhile, a dim coupling has been underway. The dimness clears: Derek and Cat sit side by side on the bench, blankets wrapped

Cat The snow's stopped.

Derek Yes.

Cat I'm sorry.

Derek I could start digging us out.

Cat No hurry.

Derek No. I love my love with an F because she is full of feeling. I hate her because she is faithless. Her name is Frances and she comes from Finland.

Cat Why do you say that?

Derek Because the female condition is common to all and you might as well be Frances from Finland. Faithless, all.

Cat I might not be.

Derek If you will with me you might with anyone.

Cat There's no way out of that one, ever.

Derek Do you feel bad?

Cat Not at all.

Derek Don't you have any feelings for Anne? You lived in her house, you understood her ways.

Cat I could never understand her saucepans. Mean, thin-bottomed things——

Derek And now you've taken what's rightfully hers.

Cat I don't think I took, I think I accepted what was offered.

Derek There can be two ways of looking at that.

Cat I don't think excuses are needed. She took a thousand pounds and stepped into my shoes, and I stepped into hers and this is what happened.

Derek You begin to look like her. Muffled up in wool.

Cat Do you like that?

Derek Yes.

Cat Why?

Derek It's familiar. It's going to be hard for me to get up to London.

Cat Why should you want to get up to London?

Derek To see you.

Cat Oh.

Derek You want to see me again. You'll want to see me quite a lot, I imagine. It seems to me you need me quite a lot. You cried.

Cat Did I?

Derek I think you're very unhappy as you are. I think that has to change. I think you're living a superficial life, but you're not a superficial person.
Cat Are we running off to Portugal together then?
Derek I think running is out of the question. I think turning and facing is more like it. I don't think you should go back to London at all. What have you got to go back to? A hairdresser's appointment?

Sounds of the snow-plough and workmen approaching

Cat (*at the window*) I think you are taking too much for granted. A few tears from me do not amount to a lifetime's remorse.
Derek You said you loved me.
Cat Under the influence of passion. And the cold. It was very draughty. You feel yearnings when you're cold. You think it's love, or forever, or God, or anything: but actually, it's just an extra blanket you need. Look, here comes the boring girl from *Femina*. Properly dressed for the snow too. Canary yellow wellies.
Derek She isn't boring. You find too many things boring. Down here you will learn a proper appreciation of people and events.

He opens the door

Derek Come in, the lady from *Femina*.

The girl from Femina *is twenty-five, lean, angular, beautiful and frizzy-haired.*
Lynn

Lynn They flew me in by helicopter. The features editor went crazy. But when I explained why he agreed. Well, he had to. It doesn't look too good for the magazine, does it? We're half-way through the feature, we've had her story and your story, and frankly it hasn't been the most exciting copy of the year. You've both grinned and bore it and said nice things about the other. I told him the life-swap story was just about played out. Had been, in fact, since those two Greenwich Village cookies swapped everything including thrush, and we can't even use sex over here. Well, *Forum* could, or *Fiesta*, but not *Femina*. We're too nice. Now your precious partners have really blown it, and we're right down in the porn area, and the editor's blaming me.
Cat I'm sorry. Could you talk a little slower? We've been rather quiet in here for some time and it's hard to follow.
Lynn Snow in March. There's something really screwy happening to the weather. I don't blame Anne, mind you. I couldn't stick it down here. All right for the men, who like to commune with nature, it's the women who really suffer. My God, I suppose you don't know and I've got to break it to you. The phones are cut off. I forgot that. Your wife has gone off with your husband. They rang the editor to say so. Which makes it either the big story of the year, or the biggest non-story. Personally, I'm banking on non-story. Heterosexual sex is so drearily predictable, I just can't believe anyone's interested.
Cat Mark gone off with Anne?
Lynn If you ask me it's some kind of exhibitionist freak-out. It's what

happens when you turn the cameras on ordinary folk, and we had no business doing it. I told the editor so, but he's no better than some kind of rapist himself. Look, as a gesture, it's not exactly going to take the world by storm, not when you consider our circulation. But for you two, yes, I guess it's a real world shaker, isn't it?—so as I said, I'm sorry.

CURTAIN

ACT II

SCENE 1

The Farmhouse Kitchen and City Apartment

The farmhouse kitchen is where the shop was: the apartment where the studio stood. Cat's in the kitchen making bread, dressed in woollies and wellies, and Anne's in the apartment, skimpily dressed and painting her toenails and looking at a copy of Queen

Presently Derek comes into the kitchen with a carrier full of elderflower blossom (or seasonal equivalent: nettles may have to do) for home-made wine which he sits and prepares. No word is spoken

At some time Mark slips into the apartment: Anne pours him a drink. Mark takes up a copy of Playboy, *and flicks through it, feet up*

Derek You're well wrapped up.
Cat Of course I'm well wrapped up. I'm cold.
Derek It's June. Summer.
Cat Is it?
Derek It'll warm up by July.
Cat And dampen down by August, I expect.
Derek Don't live your life before you've had it.
Cat Is that an old Devon saying?
Derek No. A word of advice, my love. Inter-county.
Cat You're right. I'm sorry.
Derek See how pliable you're getting! And you look so nice. Even in wellies, you don't plod. I never liked to say so, but Anne plodded.
Cat Mark used to complain I paced. Did Anne ever say she was sorry?
Derek No. Sometimes she thought it but she never said it.
Cat You won't let me go back to being mean and miserable, will you?
Derek You were never mean and miserable.
Cat I felt it, with Mark. Exercised in body, but not in soul.
Derek Aren't you making that dough too dry?
Cat No.
Derek Anne used to make it much wetter.
Cat Anne used to make a Grant loaf.
Derek How do you know?
Cat From the state of the recipe book. I make ordinary wholemeal.
Derek It's delicious.
Cat There's a terrible smell of cat.
Derek That's the elderflower wine.

Cat Does it taste like that when it's made?
Derek No. It tastes like nectar.
Cat Are you happy?
Derek Yes. Are you?
Cat Yes. I hate it.
Derek Why?
Cat Because something might go wrong.
Derek You weren't happy with Mark and something did go wrong.
Cat No. That was going right. Do you think they're happy?
Derek I hope so.
Cat That's because you're nicer than me. I hope they're unhappy.
Derek Haven't you kneaded the dough enough?
Cat No.
Derek Anne never kneaded it. She said it was not necessary.
Cat That's because she was making a Grant loaf, and denying herself the
   pleasure.
Derek To be fair, she didn't have all that much time.
Cat She had as much and as little time as I do.
Derek She had the hens as well.
Cat Hens don't take up all that much time.
Derek They do in winter. You have to wrap up warm to go out in the cold
   and put on your wellies and find the torch. You have to break the ice on
   their water. You have to remember to do it night and morning, or the fox
   gets them.
Cat Well. I forgot. And the fox got them. I'm sorry.
Derek It's my fault. I should have reminded you. Our first week. A terrible
   sight. I'm glad you didn't see it. Feathers and blood. When you've reared
   birds from infancy—warmed the chicks by the fire—fed them vitamins . . .
   well, never mind. It happened. C'est la vie. Not your fault, my
   love.
Cat My only regret is the fox got them, we didn't. All that free-range flesh
   gone to waste.
Derek I could never have eaten them! Never, Cat.
Cat And if you work out the cost of the eggs, they did come to about thirty p
   each.
Derek Anne and I worked it out at two p.
Cat You didn't include the outlay on the hen-house.
Derek Didn't we?
Cat Can't have. Now about central heating. Living by bits and pieces the
   way we do costs if anything more. The fan heater in the bedroom, the oil-
   stove in the bathroom, coal fire in the living-room, wood-stove in the
   dining-room, and solid-fuel Aga in here, comes to a good deal more than
   central heating.
Derek We'd need three thousand pounds.
Cat Then we borrow it from the bank.
Derek And central heating gives you colds. It's bad for the mucous
   membranes.
Cat Who says so?

Derek Anne.

Cat There you are. She had a vested interest in keeping you cold and miserable. I want you to be warm and happy and live for ever because I love you. I want you to go to the bank tomorrow.

Derek Will you come with me?

Cat Of course.

Derek But what about the shop?

Cat We will need an assistant in the shop.

Derek The shop can't possibly afford an assistant. You know that.

Cat Thanks to our small notoriety, thanks to people waiting just to see the expression on our faces, and forgoing the pleasure of a bus drive to Exeter on that account, the shop is actually, for once, in profit. And if we did away with the health foods and stocked confectionery it would do even better. The appetite for junk food round here is amazing.

Derek You mean Mars bars?

Cat That sort of thing.

Derek But sugar's so bad for people's teeth. You don't understand, Cat. It's not just a shop I'm running here, it's a service to the community. It's educational.

Cat Who said so?

Derek Anne.

Cat Screw the educational: why not make some money? Give to charity, if you feel bad.

Derek Don't use that kind of language. Don't throw words around like weapons. It upsets me. I like you gentle and loving.

Cat I'm sorry. If the country needs you to educate them they can employ you back at the town hall.

Derek No. That's all behind me. Office life didn't suit me. And don't say who said so, and make me reply Anne, I am beginning to feel upset, and then the wine will be a failure.

Cat How can you being upset affect the wine?

Derek It won't ferment properly.

Cat I expect if you actually cried into it, and your tears were profuse enough, and salt enough, that might effect the fermentation but otherwise what you're saying just isn't scientific.

Derek You'll learn.

Cat Am I being too brisk and competent for you?

Derek Yes.

Cat I'm sorry.

Derek I love it when you say you're sorry. It makes me feel powerful. Are you happy?

Cat Yes.

Derek It was all rather forced upon us.

Cat I know. Never mind.

Derek And I'm still not—well, I do what I can. I am learning, thanks to you. Aren't I?

Cat What you possibly lack in staying power, my dear, you make up for in attack. And you are very affectionate, and loving, and that is what I have always missed. I had a phone call about the goats, today from a Mrs Murray. She wants to buy them.

Derek Mrs Murray! She sleeps in the goat house while her goats sleep in the kitchen. Everyone knows that. She says they need the warmth; she doesn't.

Cat I love my love with a G because he is a goat. Then that's good: the goats will be going to a good home.

Derek They can't go to Mrs Murray. No. It isn't right to treat animals as human. It goes against God's plan.

Cat After we've dealt with the goats we'll get round to God.

Derek I don't understand.

Cat Never mind.

Derek I don't want the goats to go. When it comes to it, I don't. I know I complained about them, but I'm used to them, Cat.

Cat But my dear, your thighs are always black and blue from their horns. Where they've butted you.

Derek Not butted. Just pushed. Goats have very hard foreheads, you know.

Cat Yes. I had noticed. When you had flu, and I had to take them to the field. Goats are very interesting. They engage you in a kind of cosmic struggle, and yet you know they love you. I understand that. And why people go to such lengths to please them.

Derek Anne just thought the milk was good for the children. She didn't understand, as you do. So much she didn't understand.

Cat And you see, the constant pain in your thighs may be responsible for some of your sexual difficulties.

Derek You'd go so far as to describe them as difficulties, Cat? You really would? That's terrible.

Cat Not really. Difficulty is putting it strongly. I certainly don't want some kind of sexual athlete. But there is a clinic in Bristol they say is very good.

Derek Bristol! That's miles.

Cat It's not that far. It's not a foreign country.

Derek It is Avon, Cat. I don't travel much.

Cat There's an advantage in distance. No-one would know. No-one would see. But I do think the first step might be just to get your thighs back in working order.

Derek I suppose Mrs Murphy's might be a solution. How much did she offer?

Cat She didn't mention figures. I said you'd ring back. And Derek, double the figure you first think of, my dear.

Derek goes to the telephone. He dials

Derek Where are the children? Isn't school over?

Cat They went straight to your mother's.

Derek But she gives them white bread sandwiches with raspberry jam.

Cat Their favourite. So? Anne left them. They have me, now. And your mother, of course.

SCENE 2

The City Apartment

Mark surveys a double-page spread in Playboy

Mark Would you believe that?
Anne Probably not.
Mark Look.
Anne I'd rather not.
Mark Why? Jealous?
Anne Yes.
Mark Aren't you ashamed of being jealous?
Anne No.
Mark It's a despicable emotion.
Anne That's what men say. It's all a question of definition, of course. I'm in love, you're possessive, he's jealous. I love my love with an M because he's mine. Well, why not? Mine.
Mark Have you been to a solicitor yet?
Anne No.
Mark Why not?
Anne I've been too busy.
Mark What doing?
Anne I was having my hair streaked: a whole head not a half-head, and that takes forever. And they charged me for some pastrami at the delicatessen and didn't put it in the bag and then had the nerve to say I didn't pay, and your mother rang.
Mark What did she want?
Anne She wants to come and live with us.
Mark There isn't room.
Anne We may have to move to a larger place.
Mark You don't want that.
Anne She's a poor old lady, Mark. She has bad arthritis.
Mark She's putting it on. Cat used to say she was putting it on.
Anne I'm sure Cat did.
Mark She'll have changed her mind tomorrow. She doesn't want to live with me, any more than I want to live with her.
Anne Why not?
Mark She disapproves of me.
Anne Now you're with me, she might not.
Mark I don't want you getting on too well with my mother.
Anne Why not?
Mark Just think, Anne. There'd be no privacy. We need privacy, you and me.
Anne I suppose you're right. Yes. Well, we'll think of some compromise. And then your son's headmaster rang.
Mark Cat's son's headmaster. I have very grave doubts about David being my son. He might be anyone's. You know what she was like.

Anne Don't confuse the issue, Mark. David wants to come back at the
weekend. The school psychiatrist says it's essential. He's wetting the bed.

Mark Why doesn't he go down to Devon, to his mother?

Anne There isn't a washing machine down there.

Mark No washing machine? How did you manage?

Anne Very well. Derek's mother and I used to do it on Mondays in the boiler.
We had an electric wringer. And we'd hang it out on the line and God's
good fresh wind would dry it and the smell was so fresh and lovely.

Mark You're not regretting anything?

Anne No. I needed those sensual satisfactions because others were lacking.

Mark But they're not now?

Anne Oh no.

Mark You're so prudish. I love that. It turns me on. What is this about
God's fresh wind? Do you know how winds are produced? It has to
do with air pressure not God.

Anne What has it got to do with air pressure? Exactly?

Mark I'm not sure. Something.

Anne Very well. Let me say God. It doesn't do you any harm and it pleases
me.

Mark So. Between the hairdresser and the delicatessen you've agreed to have
my mother live here and Cat's son back every weekend wetting the bed.

Anne Not every weekend. Every other weekend. These are realities, Mark.
One is much happier facing them. And perhaps we ought to have a bigger
house. It is very little here.

Mark It's all we need. You and me.

Anne You and me is adolescent. The grown-up world is full of obligations.
Do you think we ought to go jogging?

Mark Physical exercise exhausts me.

Anne I hadn't noticed.

Mark Sex is different.

Anne It might make it even better.

Mark Do you think so?

Anne They say so. That's why people do it.

Mark I thought it was for their health.

Anne That's only secondary.

Mark Perhaps we should. But I might fall asleep in the office. Lose
concentration.

Anne Silly old office.

Mark What did you say? You mustn't ever say that. The office provides all
this. It gives me my status. It's the meaning in my life. What do you do,
people say? I'm in advertising, I reply. It gives me definition.

Anne Don't I give you meaning? Don't I define you? And I've never heard
anyone say what do you do for a living, because the only people we ever
meet are in advertising, and they know what you do, and how good you
are. I bought some jogging gear. Red. Velvet.

Mark Velvet?

Anne Very sensuous.

Mark Is it healthy?

Lightning Source UK Ltd.
Milton Keynes UK
UKHW021307290519
343529UK00008B/539/P